# OLD CARS & ROOTBEER

John Michael Bailey

**No. 9 Media Partners**

Copyright © 2023 John Michael Bailey

All rights reserved

The characters and events portrayed in this book are fictitious. Any similarity to real persons, living or dead, is coincidental and not intended by the author.

No part of this book may be reproduced, or stored in a retrieval system, or transmitted in any form or by any means, electronic, mechanical, photocopying, recording, or otherwise, without express written permission of the publisher.

ISBN-979-8-9888428-1-1

Cover design by: No. 9 Media Partners

Printed in the United States of America

*To my family without whom I would be nothing.*

# CONTENTS

Title Page
Copyright
Dedication
Introduction
Prologue: Who Am I And Why Am I Writing This Book?   1
The Automobile is Born   6
Where Did the Frame on Body Come From?   10
The Beginning of The Use of Iron and Steel   15
Impact of Force on the Traditional Car   19
THE UNIBODY FRAME CAR HOW IT IS BUILT   23
How Impact Affects Occupants in A Unibody Automobile   31
In Conclusion   41
Afterword   43

# INTRODUCTION

I am writing this book and the others that will follow in this series as a way to share the knowledge I have gained in about 45 years of practicing law. The general public tends to be entirely too trusing of insurance companies and adjusters who use language that the ordinary person never uses to confuse and to take advantage. With this series of books I will show and share what I know and the tricks tactics and secrets the insurance industry doesnt want you to know about. My enduring hope is that the person who finds themselves needing to know this information can read the book and gain a level of understanding of the process and how to protect themselves from the predatory behavior of the insurance industry. If you would like to know more please visit the resources on our web site, https:\\www.calljmb.com, or call us at 888-WE FIGHT. We are happy to chat with you at any time. Many thanks for stopping by and I hope you found your visit helpful. As always, I hope to talk to everyone real soon-jmb

# PROLOGUE: WHO AM I AND WHY AM I WRITING THIS BOOK?

Hi there! My name is John Michael Bailey. I'm an attorney in Memphis, Tennessee. I've been practicing law for a long, long time. I have been representing people since I was 22 years old, and in my second year of law school, and I will be 69 years old this August so for however, many years that is that's how long I've been practicing law.

This book is going to be the first in a series of about 10 I think on how property damage is important in your injury case because it is how we determine the mechanism of injury. We must determine and be able to show and prove the mechanism of injury because the number one thing that any insurance adjuster or defense counsel is going to do is try to prove that the injured person is a liar and cannot be believed. I'm going to start this series, just explaining basic things. If you have any questions about anything in the book, please reach out to us. I'll be more than happy to go over stuff or explain things more, but we have to start somewhere so let's begin at the beginning.

I want to go back to my own childhood. And one of my most vivid memories of my grandmother, my father's mother, who had a 1951 Chevrolet two door. It was a Styleline Deluxe. (four-year-old me remembers this just like it was yesterday)

I remember my grandmother when I stayed over at her house, putting us in the front seat of the car and her car had seatbelts, which was for a 1951 automobile quite unusual. Probably the earliest active safety restraint or safety system rather that was used. Nonetheless, she put me in the front seat of this car. We then drove down Getwell Road to Frost Top Root Beer, a hamburger joint. She would take me in there and get me a little something to eat but that's not the real reason we went there. Of course, I do not remember at all what we ate there, but I sure do remember the soda fountain. Fresh Frost Top root beers drawn out of the old timey soda fountains and served in frosted cold mugs. That memory is just indelible to me. I can tell you how cold the mug was on my fingers and how the smell of the root beer came up out of that glass.

I can also describe to you how the head of that root beer tickled my upper lip and how good it tastes.

And I think right then in there, began my love affair with old cars. Let me just go ahead and confess that it's a love affair that never ends. But that entire memory to me represents my grandmother loving me. I felt very safe and very secure in that car, and I felt very safe and very secure with my grandmother.

Another thing my father taught me was how to identify different cars when I was a little boy. We would be going down the street, he would point to a car and would ask me what kind of car that was. I would be able to tell him the year, the model, and the make of the car. That went on from as long as I can remember probably until I was probably in the second or third grade.

So, the time from the 1950s until maybe the mid-60s is remembered very very vividly. I'm a very big fan of those cars and how they were made.

So today cars are made very, very differently. Even though I believe in my heart, that cars that were made during our grandparents' time, were sturdier. I do believe that the cars that we drive today, even though I'm not a fan of how they're built necessarily, they are safer than the cars that we rode in back in those days. Now this is my very first book and just an introduction to more things to come. What I'm going to talk about is the difference between how cars were made then and how they are made now. Back then, on the older cars,

we called it body on frame construction versus what's now called unibody or monocoque construction.

So, without further ado and without me boring the life out of

OLD CARS & ROOTBEER

everybody taking you down memory lane. Let's go ahead and get started.

# THE AUTOMOBILE IS BORN

Even though I just promised everybody that I wouldn't go back down memory lane, I'm going to have to break that promise just a little bit. Let's go back to what I call the evolution of how cars were thought about and how they were made. If you do any type of reading or studying on the history of the early automobile industry, you'll know that for many, many years they were called a horseless carriage and that's because they were built like the carriages that were pulled by horses. So, in your mind's eye, think of when you saw a Western movie with a buggy or somebody in a covered wagon going across the West, you would have two yolks, which would be long pieces of wood.

And in between those yolks would be horses, oxen or whatever is pulling up the wagon bar that you would have a platform supported by two or four wheels that were attached to a frame. Then on top of that, there was a seating area and usually in the back, open area to carry cargo goods, supplies, that kind of stuff. You can watch any Western show or movie, and you'll see these things all through them. They're an essential part of showing what life was like back in those days.

When the gentleman, who began the modern car industry, began to try to propel these automobiles, these conveyances were the things they had to start to work with since the carriages were already in existence. If you go back and you look at pictures of the old Daimler Benz, the very first car which was made in Germany, or even the early Ford models, you will see it is basically a horseless carriage, with an engine in the front and sometimes very simple.

To operate the controls, these conveyances basically had a seat perched on top of a frame just like the old buggies or the covered wagons. As cars got more sophisticated, the materials improved and more creature comforts were added, but at the very beginning the creature comforts were few and far between. So back in the day, cars began with a very solid frame and body attached to them.

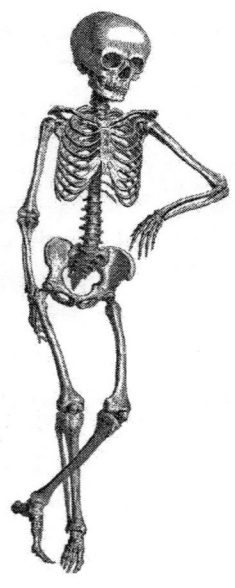

Today, we have a situation where the body of the car is the frame of the car, think in terms of a mammal versus an insect. I know that sounds crazy, but I'm going to make it sense of it all. A mammal, like us humans, has a skeleton and on top of our skeletons, our body sits. Our body is attached to our internal frame. Just like a car was probably made through the mid to late 60s.

An insect wears its skeleton on the outside and the soft and vulnerable parts of the body are contained inside the exoskeleton.

So, if you want to think in terms of biological differences between the way old cars were made and the way new cars are made. Let's think of mammals versus insects. On a mammal, if a vulnerable part is damaged, like if you hurt your arm or something like that, you can fix that. On an insect, if the exoskeleton is crushed, there's no way to prepare that.

We ran into that same situation in the new car with the unibody and monocoque construction and how these forces impact. We can prove this by going through the different types of automobiles and how it has an effect on the human beings inside of them different greatly.

We must understand the difference we have in the automobiles and understand how this force that travels through the automobile we are occupying, in order to show the mechanism of injury. It also teaches us where to look for hidden damage within the automobile. More importantly than that, where to look for hidden injuries in our bodies. So, with all this put together, let's begin with Chapter One.

# WHERE DID THE FRAME ON BODY COME FROM?

The body frame method of building cars is sometimes called the ladder frame.

All this goes back to what we went over before, to how people viewed the ability to convey human beings and their belongings. Or based upon what was available at the time automated automobiles began to be produced. Again, that was the wagon, and the wagon was built by laying out two frames, one on either side, running crossmembers in between them to give a good solid basis. Now under that, they would mount axles and wheels. On top of that they would put a flooring and put some sort of rudimentary seats, and behind that the open area.

Now we really don't refer to that part of an automobile as a ladder frame or anything like that. Those of us who do look at property damage use the word frame and a better word for that would be chassis. What that means is its solid metal on either side, again with crossmembers either bolted in or welded in. To give a good rigid backbone to the car and before everything else is added.

Now different types of automobiles can have different types of frames. If we want to travel with very very heavy loads, then we can make the frame or chassis very very heavy. This makes the Gross Vehicle Weight (GVW) very high on 18 wheelers and commercial vehicles, which is very important when we discuss how force from an impact, from such a vehicle, differs than from a regular car. That's the subject of another book. For now, let's just remember that they are indeed very heavy, some as heavy as a loaded Boeing 707. That's the reason why on the highways there are weigh stations where the trucks have to be weighed to make sure they are within the weight limits.

When I was younger, I worked at a Mack truck dealership, Tri-State Mack here in Memphis. I was able to look and see how Mack Trucks were built and put together. I can tell you that they had steel beams that ran down both sides, and all these steel beams were generally attached with great big lag bolts. Most of the time welded and upon that, they would put the cab, attach the fifth wheel to pull the trailer, and put on all the steering equipment.

I know that Ford for several years advertised their trucks as Twin I-Beam Suspension, touting that type of construction. Ford touted the many benefits of the new front suspension system: rugged construction, smoother ride, and better control. This was to prove just how tough the trucks were and how much of a heavy load that they could carry.

I don't recall seeing any cars made, after say the 1930s, that were any of the ordinary everyday cars, that had beams of steel. They had chassis made of either stamped or cast iron or later flat rolled steel plates upon which were placed the cross members. Upon that was placed the body of the car.

Okay, so let's get back to how a frame was constructed and how that became the core strength of the entire automobile. The first thing we must talk about is the design of the frame. And again, we must go back to the horse drawn carriage.

When the people who began building cars started to think of how they wanted to build them. They went back to what they knew which was again, the horse drawn carriage and again if you look at the older cars, you see in the picture above, it just looks like a carriage but without the horse.

So, what did we use or what did they use when they were building this? They started out with wood because wood is what they had. But once they realized that they needed things to be very, very durable and strong, they had to re-evaluate how they were building them. You must remember when cars were made in the beginning, we really didn't have good roads. Most of the streets in the cities were paved with cobblestones.

That's particularly true in Europe. A lot of the streets in Europe, even today are paved with cobblestones here in the United States. As I'm sure you know, from watching westerns and such, it was all dirt roads. The roads that we did have were bad and mainly just trails. I know here in Memphis, one of our busiest streets, Lamar, which actually turns into highway 78, which then turns into highway 22, began as an old Indian trading trail so the roads were terrible.

One of the things that can happen is if a piece of wood takes a hard jolt, it can snap crack or break. So very shortly after realizing this, they began using steel for the frames. Now, if you think back in history, to when all this began, it was early in the 20th century. So, by the 1900s and the 1910s, that is when cars really started being built.

# THE BEGINNING OF THE USE OF IRON AND STEEL

This caused a lot of changes in our society. One of the things that it caused was the industrial explosion in the north. This is where Bethlehem Steel and all these other steel manufacturers really started having to produce steel. It was then sent to Detroit, to the foundries there, where it was pressed, stamped, welded, whatever they needed to do to make a metal frame for the automobiles.

But the basic design in the frame remained the same. You had two strong steel beams, or plates, or what they call channel steel pieces, which is kind of like a square piece of steel, iron, or cast iron. Then these two beams were connected by crossmembers and upon those crossmembers was placed the body. The reason why they went to steel was because of its properties to be able to withstand stress, jolts, and because it was extremely durable.

Creating the frame was very labor intensive. You had to take the iron ore that was mined and not wander off too far in the weeds here. But all of this seemed to happen in pretty close proximity, to the Great Lakes. That's our inland sea here in the United States.

Most of this trade went back and forth by ship. The iron ore was delivered to the steel mills, the steel mills refined that into ingots the ingots, went over to the factories, the factories smelted that in, formed it, beat it into the shapes that it needed, and then that was delivered to the factory floor. That's where it was riveted in a lot of cases and welded as well. This is how they built the rigid framework of the frame of the car. Think of it again as a human skeleton.

The process of mining the ore needed to make the steel, the shipping of the steel, the steel workers you smelted, the ore into steel ingots, the people who are working in the foundry casting things like the frame and the engine and all the other metal parts. All of this created a huge industry in the Northeast.

When a lot of this manufacturing moved elsewhere such as Mexico or was farmed out across the globe, this led to a decline in that area. That is why sometimes now, that entire area is called the rustbelt. But that's a story for another day.

Once the frame was built, it was put on the assembly line. It would begin at one end of a massively long assembly line, and it would go down the assembly line through teams of various workers. There were specialized workers who did framing, and then there was a particular team of people who would attach axles to the frame or attach crossmembers.

Specifically, there was another assembly line that assembled the body and when it was in a position, to be able to be put on the frame at the conclusion of its assembly line, it was lifted by hoists in very gently and very specifically put in the right place and then attached.

So, what this meant was then when it was in the right place, they could rivet spot weld or attach using connectors. Sometimes using reinforcing materials like metal plates to make sure that the joints that they were making could withstand all the stresses. These cars were very, very, very solidly built. In some of the older cars, if you ever get a chance, listen to the sound that's made when someone shuts the door. It's a very very solid sound showing you that the car is put together with very very solid materials.

What this means in the real world and for us, understanding the difference between cars of yesterday and the cars of today, is that the frame is one separate piece, and the body of the car is yet another separate piece. Again, if we're going with thinking that the frame is a skeleton, then the body is the flesh that sits on the skeleton.

Why is this important? Well, if you have a fender and a traditional body on frame power that needs to be replaced. You can remove that fender from the car and replace it. You don't have to do anything to affect the structural integrity of the frame.

That is totally different when it comes to the unibody or monocoque construction poor there are companies all in the marketplace that make replacement fenders and such. You can buy them from the factory, or you can buy these replacement fenders. Typically, if you look in your insurance policy, you will have collision coverage, which gives the insurance company the right to use a replacement or a used fender. Most people object to this. What the insurance company will do is, they'll go out and they'll get a used fender, or they'll get a knockoff fender as probably made more cheaply and people feel like this devalues the car.

You know what, the people are right, it does devalue the car. This is why you have a diminishing in value claim in each and every instance of a collision and damage to your car. That adjuster is not going to tell you about the diminishing of value in a claim. But it's there. You must know about it and need to protect yourself. You have to stand up for your rights when fighting a claim. This is part of the reason why I'm writing this book.

# IMPACT OF FORCE ON THE TRADITIONAL CAR

Alright let's talk about how an impact affects a traditional body on the frame of a car and most importantly how it affects the people inside.

Modern scientists will tell you that even though modern cars are made of stronger materials and because of design, you're safer. I'm not a scientist. I'm a lawyer. I've looked at a million car wrecks (figuratively speaking) and I'm not sure about that.

Let me explain why. If you look at cars that are a traditional body on framed cars, they have a bumper that's made from steel, that is generally chromed.

So, when a car runs into the back end of that chrome bumper, they're hitting steel, not Styrofoam. Yes, I said Styrofoam. That is what's behind a crash absorbent.

In modern cars, sitting behind the bumper, Styrofoam is the same thing that they make the cheap disposable coolers out of that you take to the beach.

But back to the impact on a car with a steel bumper. That impact will travel along the frame and the force of that impact will travel through the frame into the seating frame and will propel the occupant forward and then back.

Here's where the modern construction truly is safer than in the older frame on body cars. And that's how the interiors of the occupant space are designed and built, then the cars that were on the road when I grew up.

They were more concerned with appearance, convenience, and marketing of the occupant space instead of the safety and as a result, there are a lot of hard, shiny surfaces. The dashes were made from metal.

There are a lot of knobs that protruded the steering wheel column did not collapse so when that force came through if you were the driver your chest could be impaled upon the steering column.

If you are a passenger your face could bounce off a steel dashboard, if you are a child in the backseat, you could be thrown through the windshield of the car.

I remember these are the days before mandatory seatbelts. Many children were in a front-end collision, in which the impact could cause serious and severe damage. That's why my grandmother having the seatbelts in her 1951 Chevrolet was remarkable. It was a special-order item that most people didn't deal with at all.

This is not to say that there weren't some safety issues built into the cars. The firewall for instance, was designed to absorb the force of impact of the radiator. The bracing for the radiator was also designed to absorb impact from a side impact. Because of the strength and sturdiness of the steel and other materials that were used in the construction of the doors, these likewise provided protection upon impact.

So, these cars were not automatically death traps but were built to the safety standards of that day. We have higher safety standards in cars today. They have padded dashes, airbags, and things like that. That's pretty much a description of how the frame on body cars are built from the old days til today.

As you can see things were very different then. I like the solid frame on the older cars, but I will admit that we are much safer inside the cars that are built today than we were in the interiors of the cars built in the past. Now let's turn to how cars are made today and how impact affects the integrity of those cars. Most importantly, how that impact affects the occupants of the cars.

# THE UNIBODY FRAME CAR HOW IT IS BUILT

If you have been paying any attention to what I've been saying, you know by now that I tend to wander when I'm trying to find ways to explain these concepts to people. I think it's due to my ADHD but I've got people who will sign Sworn Affidavits that's it's because I just can't shut up. Either way, here we go wandering again.

My mom's dad, my maternal Grandfather, flew Sopwith Camel's in the first World War.

He wasn't a flight officer, due to getting kicked out of officer's training because he punched an instructor. I guess fighting runs in the family. He worked on the planes as much as he flew them, so he could explain to us all manner of things from how the planes were put together, to how the machine guns worked, how they could fire without hitting the propeller, and what it felt like to fly in an open cockpit.

I can remember quite clearly myself and my first cousin, Andy, sitting on the glider on their front porch. We would listen raptly to his stories and watch him hand roll his cigarettes. I know that he might have felt like he got stuck babysitting since while our grandmother and mothers went out shopping, but I can tell you we thought it was a grand time every time we got the chance to visit with him.

The planes he flew had an internal truss and over that a cloth covering. All the strength of the airplane comes from the internal structure of the trusses, not the body of the plane itself. It's actually from this time that the concept of monocoque construction arose. Monocoque is French for "one shell" and it was first seen in a racing airplane in 1912. So, the concept has been around for more than a hundred years. Maybe the most famous example of the monocoque construction airplane would be the British mosquito fighter bomber of of World War 2.

It was light and strong and sleek and aerodynamic and it had high ratios of strength to weight and because of its streamlined design and light weight it could go very fast and had an impressive range. Impressive range as in it got great gas mileage.

So, it's from the aircraft industry that the design spread to the automotive industry. It's not that hard of a stretch for that to happen after all virtually all the automotive factories during the second world war produced aircraft or aircraft parts. What they found was that lighter more malleable materials could be stretched over a form or into a specific shape, joined together to make a frame that was light in weight but yet still retained very high strength qualities.

Once it was proven that this design could withstand the rigors of combat in the air, it was only a matter of time before the design became to be used in the automotive industry. The change came about because of the gas shortages of the early 1970's and the government mandated that automobiles get much better gas mileage.

So now let's move on to discussing the automobiles of today and from now on I will use the phrase unibody because that better describes what we will be talking about.

The unibody frame of an automobile begins as a design and that design is generally cut or stamped out of high strength light weight alloys or high tensile steel or aluminum or a combination of both. It is welded together mostly by robots now, while it goes down the assembly line until it is complete. Then the engine and drive train are added, the wheels and axles and then the interior. The only other things added to the frame are the doors of the car, the hood, and trunk lid. That's it.

So, the only parts that can be damaged without cutting into the frame of the car are the doors and perhaps the wheel assemblies. Just so you know what someone is talking about if you hear these words, the front of the driver's door hangs on what is known as the A pillar and latches on the vertical frame of the B Pillar. The rear passenger door hangs on the B pillar and latches on the C pillar. In later books, we will talk about these pillars at length and how they affect the performance and protection of the occupants of the car. We will also talk about how damage to those pillars is very difficult to repair without substantial damage to the integrity of the frame of the car. The only thing added in terms of structure on a unibody is the hood. The doors, the trunk lid, or the hatchback and it's a hatchback. That's why a good way to describe the unibody is like the shell of a crab or the exoskeleton of an insect. There is no internal structure to provide strength.

A lot of experts say that this makes the car stronger because a force is transmitted in a different way and the body is a lot safer. I will say I don't necessarily agree with that, but I will say that I do believe that the insides of modern cars are safer than the older cars. Nowadays this is a more flexible design. You don't have to worry about how you're going to connect the upper part of the car to the frame, it all becomes one integrated design. Then what you do is produce a lot more designs. You're not stuck with putting engines in between the two beams or plates of steel, then building a car behind the engine. This allows you a lot more flexibility to be in design.

But one of the things we're going to talk about here is that even though they have claims of greater safety and claims better fuel efficiency if the car gets damaged, if you don't do it just right, your problem they'll never be the same again.

In an old body on frame automobile, you can cut out a fender and you can disassemble it from the frame. You can then add another fender and you have not at that point done anything to warp the frame. Or done any kind of frame damage. You haven't damaged anything that is contained internally in between the rails of the frame.

It's not that way with the unibody construction, when any part of the frame becomes warped, then the entirety of the frame is warped. When this happens, you will see that when a back end gets smashed, they will literally cut the back end off and they will weld another back end on. That is no different than cutting the frame of an old car in half and welding it together. Same thing with a side impact, it will never ever be the same. That part of the frame tends to warp which means that the entire frame will warp.

I want you to take a piece of paper and hold it in your hand when I'm explaining this to you. I want you to twist it. Hold it in between your thumbs and forefingers and hold it straight out at a perfectly level flat piece of paper.

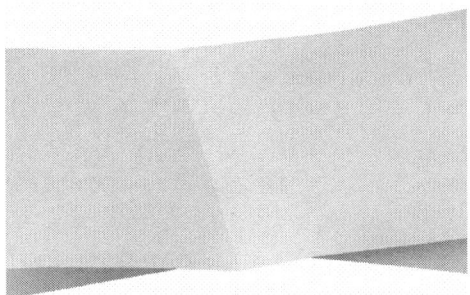

Imagine that to be the frame of unibody core. I want you to rotate one of your thumbs towards you. And I want you to rotate the other thumb away from you. And when you do that, you will see that the piece of paper twists and deforms. Even if you take it and straighten it back out it will never be the same flat sheet of paper ever again. It does the same thing with a unibody frame car when it's hit and suffers an impact.

Not only that, the unibody car does not have the internal skeleton that can protect things like your steering, your motor mounts, or your engine.

Once they are hit, for instance head on or in the wheel well, your engine will never run right, and your car will never steer right. So, everything in your car, everything, every system, every everything is subject to being hurt. If you get a rear end collision, your motor mounts might become broken and dislodge. The motor from where it is supposed to be if you are ever front-end collision then the engine and transmission might become impacted causing damage to both and so your engine will never run right, and your transmission will never shift the way that it's supposed to shift.

I don't mean just you personally, but I mean most people will trust the adjuster to do the right thing and that is the number one mistake. The adjuster just looks for the damage that can be seen. They never ever ever look for the hidden damage because they are trained not to do that. So, your car just won't ever be the same and be worth the same money as it was right before the impact. So, everything in your car, and every system in your car is subject to never working correctly again if you get in a rear end collision. Your drive motor mounts might become broken and dislodge from where it is supposed to be. If you ever have a front-end collision, then the engine and transmission might become impacted causing damage to both. Your engine will never run right, and your transmission will never sway the way that it's supposed to shift, the only thing added in terms of structure on a unibody is the hood. The doors the trunk lid, or the hatchback and it's a hatchback. So, it's very much like a little insect living down the road.

You will most certainly have a diminishing in value claim. I'll talk about that later too. But that adjuster is never ever, ever going to let you know. You'll find out about that when you take your car to trade it in and there's a CARFAX on your car.

You will find you might owe $15,000 on what you think of as a $25,000 car. You might think $10,000 worth of equity in that car is not correct. That Fairfax is going to drop your value tremendously and so you will wind up owing $15,000 on a car that might be worth 9000. That's why you need to have GAP Insurance A and B you need to know about the diminution and value claim. And if you don't ask for it, you're never going to get it because that adjuster will never ever, ever tell you.

# HOW IMPACT AFFECTS OCCUPANTS IN A UNIBODY AUTOMOBILE

I'm going to talk about how an impact affects the occupants of a unibody car. We've gone over some of the internal structure and how things work on a unibody car, but we haven't really spoken about how an impact affects people who are in a unibody car. Since most of the cars that people drive today are unibody or semi unibody cars and by that, I mean pickup trucks and some SUVs. This is important information for you to know and to understand, it will help you drive, help you keep safe, help you keep your family safe, and I want you to have this information.

Let's talk about three basic types of impact.

This is a head on impact.

Lets talk about a rear end impact

let's talk about two different types of collisions from the side one of the collisions we'll talk about will be collisions into a wheel well.

The other will be a collision into a door that affects either the A pillar which is the very front part of the passenger compartment, or the B pillar, which is going to be the vertical brace that runs down from the roof to the bottom of the frame. And is in the middle of the passenger compartment.

Before we get started diving really deep into this topic, let's talk about the safety features that are now built in to unibody cars, and how it helps keep you safe and yet how sometimes these safety features can wind up hurting you as well.

We know that there's a thing called ABS which is an automatic braking system. It's pretty common these days for most cars to have it, which means that when you try to slam on your brakes, instead of the brakes locking up, they will release a little bit and then regroup. Regroup, release regrip and that helps you not have your wheels lock and slide and skid into something that helps you actually slow your car down. That's very, very helpful. That's one of the things that I always insist on being on any car that I purchase.

The next thing is the airbags, which have been a great breakthrough in safety. But at the same time, people probably don't realize that what an airbag is, is simply an inflated plastic bag which must inflate so quickly.

It is essentially inflated by a shotgun charge. In other words, something very much like a shotgun shell will explode. Because of this it sends this with great force. If your face is impacted in the right way by one of these airbags or in the case of a side airbag hitting the side of your head, it can cause severe damage to you. People hardly ever check themselves for any kind of traumatic brain injury as the result of impacts with an airbag. But anytime these airbags deploy, we automatically check, and we train our staff to check and ask all the questions to find out whether or not there might be indicia of loss of consciousness.

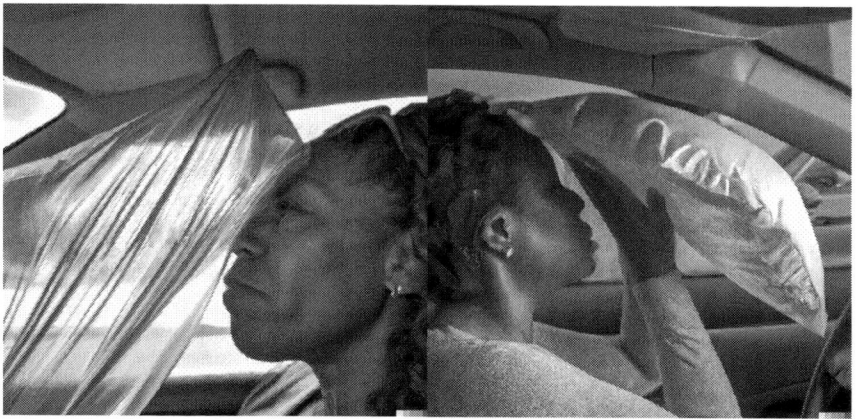

Traumatic brain injury or other injuries that could come from this impact need to be addressed in your claim.

For instance, if your chin hits the steering wheel somehow, as a result, for instance of a variant collision, or really smacked hard with an airbag, it can cause something called a temporomandibular joint syndrome injury. We call that TMJ, the jaw joint is the most used joint in the human body, and this will immediately cause damage to that.

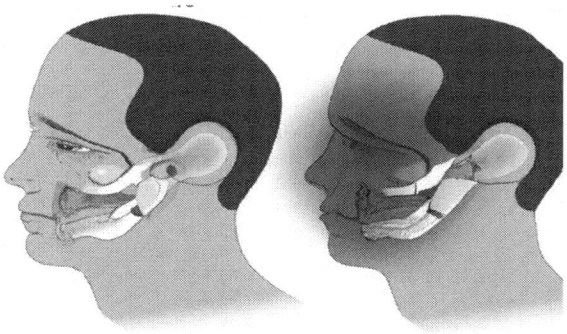

It'll knock the bite out of place and make it very very difficult for you to use. Not only that, but it will also cause incredible, incredible headaches. It's just a very unpleasant thing to have to deal with. And if you don't know how to look for the injury, you're not going to look for the injury. And if you don't go get yourself checked out for that injury, then the insurance company will never ever pay for it. Remember the insurance companies are in business to take in money and not pay it out.

Of course, with airbags impacting the face or even upper body. You always need to check for cervical injuries as well. We will talk about all kinds of injury information in upcoming books right now we're just talking about how it affects you. Let's go to the rear end collision.

The rear end collision will often propel you forward. Because there are no sensors for the front airbags in the back, a rear end collision can make your face hit the dashboard or steering wheel. You can also hit either side of the window if you're the driver or the passenger causing damage. There's something called Brain shear and again, we'll get into that in other books but that's a very, very serious injury. Again, if you don't know what to look for, you never will. With certain cars the impact will be so severe that it will cause the frame of the seat to collapse to the back of the car. That will cause a lot of injuries such as lumbar trauma, lumbar being the area of your spine, which is round your beltline. Lastly, in a rear end collision, you can bang your knees into the dashboard which is quite common particularly for the driver, the cockpits, and the seating system and in some of these smaller cars is quite tight. Those are quite common injuries. And again, you wouldn't think that your knees would hurt in a rear end collision but often they do.

OLD CARS & ROOTBEER

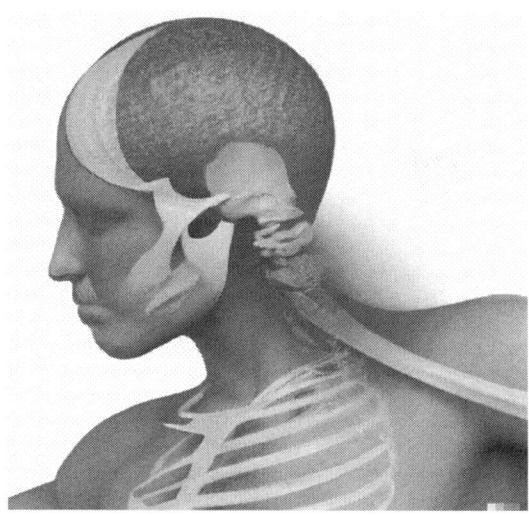

We cannot forget about the cervical issues from your body being propelled clinically forward, and then by inertia being whipped backwards. This causes hyperextension and hyperflexion of the neck. The insurance adjusters like to call this whiplash and make it like it's nothing but that's not true. There's a thing called ligament laxity, and it's a documented medical condition but of course the insurance industry doesn't want you to know about it. Basically, what that means is that once a ligament is stretched, it never ever, ever goes back to where it was. We see these kinds of injuries typically in people who are over 40, where their neck has never given them any kind of problems, but after a whiplash type hyperextension injury, they will have continued pain in the neck. This is because the ligaments held their head up straight and when the ligaments can no longer do that the muscles step in and try to accomplish the same thing by tensing up the muscles in the back and neck. This causes the pain and the aching that leads to the aching neck and even the headaches to follow that.

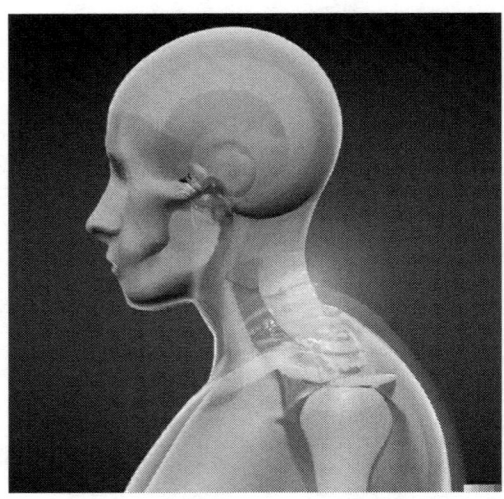

Finally, let's look at the two different types of side collisions. One is in the wheel well. And one is into the pillars of the car. Now if it's into the wheel, what's going to happen is the tire, steering knuckle, and the steering mechanism is going to absorb a lot of injury. I know that the experts say that shouldn't be dissipated throughout the entire car, but it is, so what that means is, that if you're hit in the wheel, it's not necessarily going to show the damage that was caused. You won't be able to know that unless you get into the car and start looking for the motor mounts, start checking the engine, and start checking the transmission system. You want to do that, not only because of getting your car fixed, you want to do that because that also shows the mechanism of the injury to you. Now that type of collision, you're going to see is it's going to be an oblique side to side movement which means you are moving a diagonal direction. With this, you typically see people's heads impacting with the A pillar.

What the A pillar would be from the inside perspective is the part of the door and the frame that goes around the window. So, you're going to have side to side to the neck. Again, we're going to have issues with ligament laxity and cervical issues. Now one of the things we always ask in these types of collision is for people to pay attention to what's going on with their body. If we think there'll be cervical or lumbar injury, we're going to ask you about numbness and tingling in certain parts of your body because that indicates where the trauma has occurred.

Finally, let's move on to just what we call a T bone where the front of the car just smacks into the right in the middle car. Got it? Right behind the driver's seat. That's where the B pillar is. And even though we have that vertical brace there, the car will bend like a pretzel. When that happens, you're going to have a very violent and forceful side to side collision. This means added impact on the driver's side. The driver is going to smack that window again because the sensors for the airbag may not be triggered depending on where the impact is. You can hit that glass which is going to cause all kinds of problems up to including a brain bleed or maybe a fracture. Then the inertia is going to take you flying towards the other side. We have seen many cases where two people in a car will collide with one another. That's right, they'll smack their heads together because of the way that they're being bounced around in a car.

So, all of these even with the many, many safety systems that we have, because the materials are lighter, they're not as dense as the steel that's used and the older beyond frame. There is a lot more force transmitted to people, even with all the safety issues.

# JOHN MICHAEL BAILEY

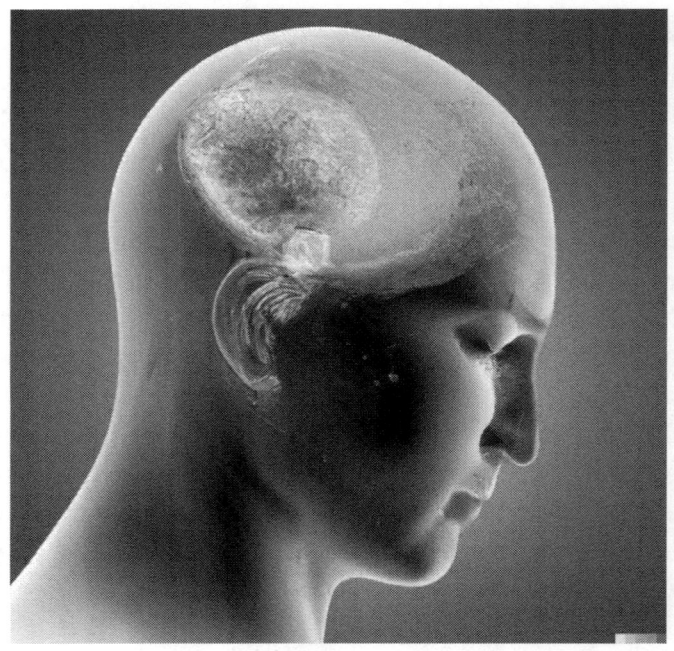

# IN CONCLUSION

So that sort of brings us to the closing of this book. We hope that you've learned many things, not just the difference between how cars are built. From the old days until today, these are things that you need to know to protect yourself if you get into a wreck.

Again, we never want anybody to be hurt but if you are hurt, we ask that you please consider calling us. We'd love to talk to you and would love to help you.

You can reach us any time at our main number 888-WE-FIGHT, and that number is good for both of our offices so no worries about that. Another way you can reach us is on the web at https: \\www.calljmb.comcalljmb.com. We would love to hear from you.

So again, thanks for taking the time to read this book. We hope it's helpful and be sure to watch for my other books that are to follow. If you see something in here that I've gotten wrong, I would love for you to reach out and tell me what it is. We want to give the best possible information to people so that they can protect themselves. Thank you all for reading and I hope that I get a chance to talk to each and every one of you very soon. All the best to you and your family,

John Michael Bailey

Attorney at Law.

# AFTERWORD

Many thanks for taking the time to read the book and I realize that I have probably raised as many new questions as I have given answers. No worries. This is the first in a series of books and I will try to cover everything in the books. But in the meantime if you have specific questions or have topics you would like for me to cover please email us at intake@calljmb.com and we will do our best to get t them answered promptly. The firm contact info is below:

John Michael Bailey Injury Lawyers
5978 Knight Arnold Road
Memphis Tennessee 38115
888- WE FIGHT

John Michael Bailey Injury Lawyers
611 Garfield Street
Tupelo Mississippi 38801
888- WE FIGHT

Made in United States
Orlando, FL
13 October 2023